Timothy Bottom's Legacy

Featuring Your Heavenly Crowns of Glory

ALAN PORTMANN

ISBN 978-1-64416-996-4 (paperback)
ISBN 978-1-64416-997-1 (digital)

Christian Faith Publishing, Inc.
832 Park Avenue
Meadville, PA 16335
www.christianfaithpublishing.com

Printed in the United States of America

This book is dedicated to our awesome first
grandchild, Lynden James, my special prodigy!

Acknowledgment

A special thank you goes to my father, Albert, who helped make this book a reality.

Contents

Foreword

Am I my brother's keeper?
—Genesis 4:9 (NAS)

The Bible describes Christians who follow Christ's doctrines in our earthly life of faith, hope, and love as obtaining heavenly crowns with diadems of glory from Christ as they enter heaven. Examples of these diadems are love, righteousness, and joy. This book endeavors to explore real-life examples of actual Christians' walk of faith, striving to achieve these crowns of glory in service to the Lord.

How do you want to be remembered after you die? Would you like to be remembered with virtues of love, compassion, integrity, and self-sacrifice, such as Mother Teresa, John Kennedy, or Dr. Martin Luther King? Or would you like to be remembered as hateful, selfish, evil, or greedy like Hitler, Stalin, or Jack the Ripper? Many people live a life of ambivalence and are soon forgotten after death because they had no positive or negative impact on others. How you live your life will determine what your legacy will be after you die. Life is all about the choices you make and how you conquer the situations you face.

This is the story of Timothy Bottom's legacy and how it manifested itself at his funeral and in the testimonials people tell his nephew, Joshua. Although the characters are fictional, the testimonials were taken from actual events in the lives of real people. Hopefully, it will give you insight into molding your legacy as others will remember it, especially children, who survive long after you die, generationally.

CHAPTER 1

The Journey

But lay up for yourselves treasures in heaven,
where neither moth nor rust destroys, and where
thieves do not break in or steal; for where your
treasure is, there will your heart be also.
—Matthew 6:20–21 (NAS)

"Do I have to go to Uncle Tim's funeral? It's a long way, and I hardly even knew him," Joshua argued.

"Yes, you must go," Joshua's mother replied as she continued to pack for the long journey across the country. "Uncle Timothy loved you so much, even though he couldn't be with you," his mother added.

Uncle Timothy's job required him to constantly travel around the globe. Joshua admitted to himself, even though he couldn't spend time getting to know his Uncle Timothy, he did faithfully send great presents on birthdays and holidays. *Well, if I must go, let's get this over with,* Joshua thought to himself. Joshua lived in Boston, while Uncle Timothy's funeral was going to be in Los Angeles, California.

The flight to Los Angeles was arduous and uneventful. Aunt Martha, Timothy's widow, was the first person to greet Joshua as he stepped off the plane with his family. She had a loud, commanding voice, and she loved to talk constantly. Aunt Martha immediately lovingly embraced Joshua's cheeks with both her hands, enthusiastically proclaiming how handsome a young man he had become. Turning red as a beet, Joshua pictured everyone at the airport glaring directly at them during this embarrassing moment.

Aunt Martha chauffeured Joshua's family to her home, where they were to stay the night. Anyone and everyone Joshua ever knew was at Aunt Martha's home that night. Even people Joshua did not know were there. Feeling alone in a room full of adults, he took comfort in knowing that he was only there for a few days. Uncle Timothy had no children, and Joshua couldn't help but wonder who this man was whom he hardly knew. Uncle Timothy's funeral was scheduled for the next day.

The first thing Joshua noticed in Aunt Martha's home was that photographs of relatives, both living and dead, inundated every room in the home. It was like observing a historical archive of Joshua's family history going back over a hundred and fifty years. Most of these photographs had names and brief descriptions of who these relatives were in life. One photograph next to Uncle Timothy's bed was a large image of Joshua taken a few years earlier. It had these words inscribed on it: "Joshua, my beloved prodigy!" Needless to say, Joshua was very curious as to why his photograph was next to Uncle Timothy's bedside and what the word *prodigy* meant. All these photographs were the topic of conversation before the funeral.

The following morning, Uncle Timothy's funeral was held. After his eulogy, Joshua noticed a long line of mourners assembled to console Joshua's family. One by one, each consoler offered their unique, impromptu testimonials of who Timothy Bottoms really was in life and what he had done for them. The following was what Joshua heard.

CHAPTER 2

Great Grandpa Harper

*You will also be a crown of beauty in
the hand of the Lord, and a royal dia-
dem in the hand of your God.*
—Isaiah 62:3 (NAS)

The first person in line to console Joshua's family was Aunt Emma. She was a meek, frail, yet kind old lady, Joshua observed. Emma's soft, gentle yet strong voice permeated the room as she seemed to be speaking directly to Joshua.

"My proudest memory of your Uncle Timothy was when we were children being allowed in a hospital room at your Great-Grandpa Harper's bedside. Children were not normally allowed in a hospital room at that time. But because Great-Grandpa Harper was dying, the doctor relented.

"The scene in the hospital room was gloomy, desperate, and sad with a sense of hopelessness in the air. Yet, overshadowing this was Great-Grandma Harper's sense of faith, hope, and love. She was a strong-willed woman used to getting her own way in life. She lovingly held Great-Grandpa Harper's hand while praying constantly over him for a healing miracle. Great-Grandma Harper would always finish her prayer requests by asking it in Jesus's name in accordance with God's will. She would softly sing Great-Grandpa Harper's two favorite Gospel songs: 'It is well with my soul' and 'Where no one stands alone.' Great-Grandma Harper was never one to show her emotions until this night," Aunt Emma observed.

"Great-Grandpa Harper smoked a pipe most of his life and had developed skin cancer on his lip which spread to his jawbone. Treatment for this cancer required portions of his face and jaw to be cut away. The smell in his hospital room reeked of decaying flesh, and visually, he looked horrible on his deathbed, albeit his pain was eased by medication.

"Your Uncle Timothy was a very young boy, not even of school age," Aunt Emma said. "After the family prepared your Uncle Timothy to see Great-Grandpa Harper, given the rancid smell in the room and his gruesome physical appearance, Timothy adamantly insisted on seeing Great-Grandpa Harper one last time.

"Timothy's mother gently took his hand and walked hesitantly into Great-Grandpa Harper's hospital room. What I observed next brought tears to my eyes," Aunt Emma said. "Timothy looked over Great-Grandpa Harper's trembling body reeking with pain and immediately tenderly held his hand and stated, 'I love you, Great-Grandpa Harper. You mean the world to me and always will!' Then your Uncle Timothy gently kissed and caressed Great-Grandpa Harper's hand. It was the only part of Great-Grandpa Harper's body that Timothy could touch, with all the wires and machines hooked up to him. As Timothy tearfully smiled, you could feel the love emanating from Great-Grandpa Harper's soul as he tried to respond.

"Great-Grandpa Harper died peacefully soon after your Uncle Timothy left the room. Immediately after Timothy found out that Great-Grandpa Harper had died, he said a prayer for him. Uncle Timothy thanked God for what time he was able to spend with Great-Grandpa Harper and stated that he would truly miss him until they meet again in heaven. Naturally, Timothy's prayer brought tears to Great-Grandma Harper's eyes, and mine. This was my fondest memory of your Uncle Timothy," Aunt Emma told Joshua's family with a heartfelt hug.

CHAPTER 3

The Tithe

Thou hast crowned the year with thy bounty.
—Psalms 65:11 (NAS)

The next person in line was an elderly woman who was a total stranger to Joshua's family. She introduced herself as Amanda. Amanda met Timothy only once, yet the meeting was life-changing to her. As if she were speaking directly to Joshua, she uttered, "Tithing comes in many forms, and not just in giving money to charities. Tithing comes in actions, words, and deeds, as well as your Uncle Timothy was acutely aware of as a young man."

Amanda stated that her grandma was a widow when Timothy first met her. She gave her testimony by first describing her grandma's personality. Amanda said, "My grandma lived alone for many years and was a very independent-minded, strong-willed woman. She liked doing things her own way and didn't take kindly to strangers." Amanda continued saying, "She kept to herself especially since becoming a widow about five years earlier. To open herself up to people was not in her nature. However, she loved reminiscing and dwelling in the good old days.

"Timothy was about twenty years old when he attended the University of Missouri, Columbia. He had no money at that time, much less to tithe with. Timothy walked everywhere he needed to go, including about two miles each way to college on weekdays from his apartment. Every weekday, he would pass by my grandma's house on a lot adjacent to the main highway in town. My grandma lived alone while we lived about fifty miles out of town.

"One night, in December, I think, a wet, heavy snowstorm hit town, causing the roads to be iced over and blanketed with snow. The city municipality required the residents to shovel their sidewalks. Residents are legally liable if someone slipped and hurt themselves on their sidewalks. Timothy was keenly aware of this.

"As Timothy was walking to the college campus to take a final exam, he passed by my grandma's snow-blanketed sidewalk. Timothy noticed my grandma trying to sweep the heavy, wet snow away from her porch—with a broom no less. Without hesitation, Timothy stopped, introduced himself to my grandma, and politely inquired as to what she was doing outside in these frigid temperatures. 'Cleaning the sidewalk of snow,' she retorted curtly. Despite being complete strangers to each other, Timothy responded, 'I'll shovel your sidewalk after I finish taking my final exam today.' My grandma responded, 'How much do you charge for this service?' Timothy replied, 'A warm cup of cocoa and some good old-fashioned fellowship is what I'm charging you.' Being a shut-in and needing the help, my grandma agreed.

"That afternoon, Timothy returned and shoveled her sidewalks, drank a cup of cocoa, and enjoyed talking with my grandma about life in the good old days. It reminded Timothy of wonderful experiences he'd had as a child reminiscing about the past with his grandparents.

"It was several months later when we visited my grandma's home and she told us all about this Good Samaritan named Timothy. During that visit, Timothy happened to check in on her to see if she needed anything and if she was okay. We finally got to meet him in person that day and told him how much we appreciated him being there for our grandma when we couldn't. We handed him a jar of grandma's homemade purple plum jelly, Timothy's favorite, and became lifelong friends."

CHAPTER 4

The Book

And when the chief Shepherd appears, you
will receive the unfading crown of glory.
—1 Peter 5:4 (NAS)

The next two people Joshua met introduced themselves as Kevin and Mike. They told Joshua that Uncle Timothy was a devout Christian who loved to write and aspired to be a published author of children's books. As children, Kevin and Mike didn't even know that Timothy, as an adult, was aware of their existence until that one special day when they got the gift of a lifetime. Here is how their story unfolded.

One day, Timothy wrote a children's book about a boy who loved to play football. In this story, the quarterback makes an embarrassing mistake that almost costs them the game. However, in the end, the coach makes the quarterback the hero saying that it's the person, not winning at all cost, that really matters in life. "Coincidentally, I was the quarterback for our high school team at that time," Kevin said. "Timothy sent this story to my parents to get their approval to dedicate this children's book to me."

Mike's dad was an artist who happened to be the high school football coach at that time. Because Mike's dad loved to draw sketches and colorful pictures, Timothy asked him to illustrate this children's book. Mike's dad agreed and was very excited to get started on his illustrations. The following week, Mike's dad died suddenly of a massive heart attack, caused by what the doctors termed "the widow-maker." Naturally, Mike was devastated at this loss. So, Timothy decided to include some sketches Mike's dad drew before he died in this children's book and dedicate the story to his dad as well. He even put a photograph of Mike's dad on a dedication page in the book!

When the book was published, Timothy surprised Kevin and Mike by taking them out to pizza and giving them an autographed copy of this children's book dedicated to them. Because Mike's dad coined the slogan "No regrets" at the school football games, Timothy also wrote the following:

Go for your dreams and you'll have no regrets.
I believe in you boys. You're the best of the best!

"Timothy told us that we were loved by many people other than our relatives, not the least of which was him. Today, this children's book is sold all over the world on the Internet. Timothy has successfully published additional children's books since then, dedicated to other children who touched his life just by being themselves in life."

CHAPTER 5

The Most Valuable Treasure

*For who is our hope or joy or crown of
exaltation? Is it not even you, in the pres-
ence of our Lord Jesus at his coming?*
—1 Thessalonians 2:19 (NAS)

The next person in line to console the family was a middle-aged woman who introduced herself as Becky. Becky had a school teacher's strict authoritarian demeanor that exuded confidence and kindness as she spoke. Once again, as if she was speaking directly to Joshua, Becky gave her testimonial of how Timothy touched her life forever. Here is what she said.

"Your Uncle Timothy was the reason I became a school teacher," Becky said. Timothy loved to volunteer at the elementary and high schools doing learning centers on specific grade-level learning skills, like compare-and-contrast skills for second graders and patterning skills for fourth and fifth graders. He would frequently include gifts for every child in the classroom. "I clearly remember your Uncle Timothy greeting the students at our classroom door, usually after last recess, with a big smile and hugs welcoming us to his learning seminar.

"On one occasion, he brought in real Civil War artifacts and made the class hard tack cooked exactly like it was during the Civil

War. Today, you can no longer bring food into the classroom, but at that time we could. Timothy helped the students experience the Civil War by observing buttons, buckles, and other artifacts from the day. He even introduced the class to a picture of the CSS *Hunley*, which was the first submarine to sink an enemy warship named the USS *Housatonic* during the Civil War.

"In another seminar, Timothy brought authentic Paleozoic relics in the classroom, like a fossilized dinosaur egg, a mastodon, a seven-inch-wide Megalodon shark teeth, and an allosaurus talon. He even had a CD-ROM where we could listen to the sounds a parasaurolophus dinosaur made based on skull X-rays that the children could look at in this seminar. Timothy said he couldn't recreate the actual music this dinosaur roared, but he could recreate the sounds it made from the hornlike extension out of its skull.

"In one seminar, your Uncle Timothy would teach the children all about the history of money. The children observed and learned firsthand about the evolution of old money from gold and silver coins to horse blanket notes and silver-and-gold certificate paper currency to present-day money. The seminar culminated in a '4-H Out' game, resulting in every child receiving a bronze mint-condition Roman coin from around the time of Christ. The winner of this game received a Morgan silver dollar and a bronze Roman coin! Timothy was a 4-H leader at that time. All the coins were identified by the emperors and the dates. The teacher would later expand on this seminar by incorporating their coin into mathematics, science, and history lessons." Becky said, "To this day, these children still have their coins and will cherish them and your Uncle Timothy's generosity always."

Each seminar that Timothy conducted started the same way. Timothy would have a large, beautifully wrapped box sitting on the counter in plain sight of everyone. On the box was a sign with two clues on it about what was in it, as follows:

1. I have something in this box. There is something in this box!

2. What you see in this box is the most valu-
    able treasure known to exist in the universe.
    It's more valuable than all the gold in Fort
    Knox!

"At the end of the seminar, the class was allowed to see what was so valuable in that beautiful box. Many children, including me at that time, had low self-esteem. Well, we took turns by rows coming up to observe what was in that box, promising not to tell what we saw until every row had a chance to look in the box. A mirror was covering the bottom of that box. When we looked inside that box, we saw ourselves. Timothy said that material things like gold can be replaced. However, we are all unique, one-of-a-kind treasures from heaven that are irreplaceable. It's what makes us all special!"

Then Becky recited using Jesus's own words in Matthew 5:16: "Let your light shine before men in such a way that they may see your good works and glorify your father who is in heaven." She added, "I remember giving Timothy a big hug for that lesson."

CHAPTER 6

The Next-Door Neighbor

Blessed is the man who perseveres under
trial; for when he has been approved, he
will receive the crown of life, which the Lord
has promised to those who love him.
—James 1:12 (NAS)

Tom was the next person in line to console Joshua's family. He was a very old man in his late eighties. He was a kind old man whose personality seemed to portray compassion and empathy as he spoke. His testimonial of how Joshua's Uncle Timothy impacted his life was as follows.

"Timothy and I were next-door neighbors about thirty-five years ago," Tom said. "I was married to my first wife for over twenty years and had just got laid off from my job at the mill in town. A few months later, my wife left me for another man who was very wealthy and had all the material things in life you could ever want. As if that wasn't bad enough, I soon received delinquent charge card bills that my ex-wife had run up in my name without my knowledge. I was on unemployment, had no money, and was saddled with five thousand dollars in overdue credit card debts. That was a lot of money thirty-five years ago, and she had wiped out all my savings before she left me. As far as I was concerned, it was the end of my world," Tom said.

"Naturally, I became bitter, angry, and withdrawn. Then a miracle happened, thanks to Timothy. Out of nowhere, Timothy knocks on my door, sits down with me, and inquires as to how I am doing. Timothy continued saying, 'I understand that you've had a large amount of unexpected debt fall into your lap, and I would like to help you.' To make a long story short, Timothy offered to pay off these overdue credit card debts."

Tom told Timothy that his debt was five thousand dollars and he couldn't possibly repay him anytime soon. Timothy said, "You don't understand, Tom. I'm offering to pay off this debt. It's not a loan." Tom, in disbelief said, "Why would you do this? I'm not even a relative of yours." Timothy reassured Tom, saying, "Because I care and am able to provide this resource for you is why I'm doing this for you." There were no contracts, lawyers, or anything involved in Timothy offer. Timothy just paid off this debt.

Again, as if speaking directly to Joshua, Tom said "Your Uncle Timothy didn't stop there. He helped me find a job as a machine operator locally that offered decent pay and good insurance. Of course, I took the job and insisted on paying Timothy back. Timothy refused to take any money from me, and we became lifelong friends. I did help Timothy do his home projects whenever and wherever I could. God bless your Uncle Timothy," Tom concluded.

CHAPTER 7

The County Fair

In the future there is laid up for me the crown of
righteousness which the Lord, the righteous judge,
will award to me on that day, and not only to me,
but also to all who have loved his appearing.
—2 Timothy 4:8 (NAS)

Bobby was a middle-aged man next in line with his testimonial. He said his fondest memories of Timothy was at the county fair when he was a child. Joshua noticed that he seemed to have a childlike personality and a boyish grin as he spoke.

"Timothy would always take the time to play with us even when he as busy presiding over the animal barn at the fairgrounds." Bobby told Joshua that Timothy treated him to a funnel cake and said, "I can take any ride you can take!"

"So he bought us two tickets to ride the Spider. This was a ride that spun constantly and rapidly, suddenly and frequently changing directions three-dimensionally, up, down, and sideways. Right after eating, we got on that ride. It didn't take but a minute or two when Timothy turned white as a sheet and got sick, saying, 'You win my challenge, Bobby.' It was the last ride he rode on the rest of that day.

"One day at the fair, the adults played Bingo for half the pot collected per game. Timothy would let us sit with him knowing that if he won the pot, he would treat us to snow cones, rides, and such afterward. Before the Bingo game ever started, Timothy would say in jest, 'Look, we're doing great! The game hasn't even started yet and we're tied for first place. We even got a free space head start.'" Bobby shook his head and laughed. But the real kicker for Bobby was when Timothy actually won a Bingo game. Speaking directly to Bobby in an excited voice, Timothy said, "Quick, yell 'Bozo.' We won!" Before Bobby could even react, he yelled, "Bozo! No, I mean Bingo."

"Everybody laughed, including myself, as Timothy gave me a hug and spent the money on us children, buying tickets for rides and snow cones with the winnings."

Bobby continued to tell Joshua that Timothy would introduce exotic animals at the fair like the Phoenix, which was a colorful bird with a yard-long tail! He taught us how to properly raise and handle the animals and gave interesting facts about them. For instance, in over 90 percent of chicken species, the color of their ears is what color eggs they lay. Then Timothy would show the children brown, blue, white, and green eggs on display at the fair barn. Timothy also showed an egg laid without a shell, which was probably due to a calcium deficiency.

He loved to tell the children silly jokes: What did the Daddy Buffalo say to his son when going off to work? The answer was, of course, "Bison!" Timothy even had a dirty joke he would tell. Why did the little boy with diarrhea suddenly leave the church service during the pastor's sermon? The answer was: because he didn't want to sit in his own pew!

"He loved to play paper football on the table in the animal barn with us in the afternoon. Timothy would teach us all about the animals and how to make paper jet and glider airplanes. After the fair was over, Timothy would teach us to use his metal detector to search for coins on the fairgrounds. Timothy would share with us the money found using that metal detector." Speaking to Joshua, Bobby said he loved Uncle Timothy and would miss him dearly.

CHAPTER 8

The Angel Tree

Thou hast loved righteousness and hated lawless-
ness; Therefore God, thy God hath anointed thee
with the oil of gladness above thy companions.
—Hebrews 1:9 (NAS)

The next person in line to console Joshua's family was a petite woman named Debbie. She was in second grade when she had first met Timothy. Christmas season was Timothy's favorite time of year. At that time of year, they had a Christmas tradition called the Angel Tree in which needy children in school would fill out their Christmas wish list and place it on the community school Christmas tree. If you were lucky enough to get your wish list picked off the tree by a Good Samaritan, your Christmas dreams could come true.

"I was an only child, and my family was very poor," Debbie stated. She lived in a run-down trailer park in a poor community at that time. "Christmas for me was an orange in my stocking, and that was about it. I idolized Disney's Cinderella and always wanted to be a princess," Debbie told Joshua. "My Christmas wish list was anything with Cinderella on it." Debbie said that she really didn't expect anyone to pick her wish list off the Angel Tree. Debbie thought she might get Cinderella crayons and color books, which would have made her Christmas.

Debbie said that in school she was teased and ridiculed for wearing old hand-me-down clothes. The other children had new modern clothes, like fluorescent glow-in-the-dark shoes. They all kept to their own groups of exclusive cliques and would play cruel tricks on her. The other school children would RSVP invitations to attend Debbie's birthday party, only to not show up. Debbie lost trust in people as a child and was very shy and withdrawn due to the constant bullying she experienced. As a child, she would usually play alone and loved pretending to be a princess in her own imaginary magical kingdom.

Well, on the last day of school before the Christmas holiday, a delivery was made to Debbie's trailer full of packages addressed directly to her! Debbie got so excited that she couldn't wait and opened the presents early. She was astonished to see a cool bicycle, complete outfits that were her size, socks, crayons, books, shoes, and toys all with Cinderella on them. Debbie said that her father was in tears as there was a present for him too. Inside a Christmas card was a gift certificate for the whole family to eat a full dinner at a nearby deluxe restaurant with all the Christmas trimmings.

It wasn't until the following year when Debbie inadvertently overheard a teacher saying who gave her family the Cinderella Christmas gifts in the hallway. Debbie told Joshua that it was none other than his Uncle Timothy. "That was the best Christmas we ever had," Debbie told Joshua.

Epilogue

I am coming quickly; hold fast what you have,
in order that no one take your crown.
—Revelation 3:11 (NAS)

There were many other testimonials given at Timothy's funeral that day. These included such things as a man whose mother was Timothy's third grade teacher, and she was so taken aback by Timothy's manners, behaviors, and kindheartedness as a child that she named her son after Timothy. There were also testimonials by people who attested to Timothy's work on their behalf in Awannas, 4-H, and Boy Scouts. There were also testimonials of Timothy randomly going to a restaurant and surprising customers by paying for the dinner tab without their knowledge.

Proverbs 16:9 states, "The mind of a man plans his way, but the Lord directs his steps." Joshua realized that Uncle Timothy was a man he could look up to. He could relate to Uncle Timothy's bedside photograph depicting Joshua as his beloved prodigy! Joshua learned that *prodigy* meant to work wonders and be generous. He finally realized, through these testimonials, that every moment in time presents an opportunity to serve God in both the big and little things of life. Joshua vowed to himself to carry on Uncle Timothy's legacy by doing everything he could to serve others and tithe in money and time for the betterment of all mankind.

Then Aunt Martha reminded Joshua of his Uncle Timothy's favorite Bible verse, Proverbs 17:6: "Grandchildren are the crown of old men. And the glory of sons is their fathers." Aunt Martha told Joshua that even though she had no grandchildren, this verse applies to nephews as well! Thanks to his Uncle Timothy, Joshua couldn't wait to get started on his legacy!

"He has told you O man, what is good; And what does the Lord require of you but to do justice, to love kindness and to walk humbly with your God" (Micah 6:8, NAS).

Moral of the Story

With life so short
and time so dear,
it's very important
in life to care!

Build your treasures in heaven,
and not on this earth.
As yeast does to leaven,
there's rewards in putting God first.
God bless you!

—Alan E. Portmann

About the Author

 Alan Portmann received a bachelor of arts in education with an emphasis in science/math from the University of Missouri, Kansas City. He recently retired from an aerospace and defense company as an engineer with thirty-two years' service. He lives on a seventy-five-acre farm in Camden, Arkansas, and has two daughters. His hobbies include fishing, gardening, and collecting antiques, which he shares with children in the classroom. He is a devout Christian whose motto at school is "Teachers have a lot of class!"

CPSIA information can be obtained
at www.ICGtesting.com
Printed in the USA
LVHW021119100119
603369LV00001B/77/P

9 781644 169964